Advent Fun for All the Family!

Patrick Coghlan

kevin mayhew

First published in 2008 by
KEVIN MAYHEW LTD
Buxhall, Stowmarket, Suffolk, IP14 3BW
Tel: +44 (0) 1449 737978 Fax: +44 (0) 1449 737834
www.kevinmayhew.com

9 8 7 6 5 4 3 2 1 0

ISBN 978 1848670457
Catalogue No. 1501116

Cover design by Dave Cullen
Edited by Katherine Laidler
Typeset by Richard Weaver

Printed and bound in Great Britain

Contents

Introduction

Advent Fun for All the Family is a creative family Bible study for Advent. It is really two books in one: *Born in my town* and *Follow the maker's instructions*. Central to both are twelve of the key characters in the nativity story. *Born in my town* looks at the first coming of Jesus and how these characters were involved. *Follow the maker's instructions* looks ahead to the second coming of Jesus and what lessons we can learn from these key characters as we prepare for that time.

Each session consists of Bible study, discussion, prayer and a creative time. The ongoing creative project contained in *Born in my town* brings the nativity story into a modern and relevant setting, encouraging a new and greater understanding of what it means to meet with Jesus this Christmas. The creative project in *Follow the maker's instructions* suggests imaginative and artistic ways of producing 'To Do' lists, as a way of actively applying what is learned from Scripture to everyday life.

The aims of *Advent Fun for All the Family* are to emphasise what Christmas is really about, to encourage us to meet Jesus this Christmas and to be prepared for his return, looking at what that means regarding our relationship with him and what we have been called to be and do in the meantime.

About the author

Patrick Coghlan is the pastor of Worstead Baptist Church in Norfolk. He has considerable experience of working with all age groups, both in the Church and in the wider community. As a Baptist minister, he provides pastoral care and teaching, regularly takes school assemblies, leads a monthly service at a sheltered housing scheme and is actively involved with a Christian community care charity.

He is also a trained Christian counsellor and an enthusiastic author. *Advent Fun for All the Family* is his twelfth book for Kevin Mayhew.

Patrick is married to June. They have two children, Rachel and Jonathan.

How to use this book

It is a good idea to read all the relevant passages of Scripture telling the Christmas story – Matthew 1:18–2:23; Luke 1:26–2:40; John 1:1-18 – before 1 December. Use a favourite version of the Bible for this, maybe even a dramatised one which would allow everyone to take an active part.

Born in my town examines the involvement of twelve characters from the Christmas story. Through a time of reading the Bible, chatting together and being creative, it seeks to enable you and your family to prepare for Christmas by highlighting its reality and application to us today.

Theme picks out a key role that the character plays in the Christmas story.

Read together gives the references for a short passage in the Bible.

Chat together consists of some discussion points which will encourage you to chat informally about the role of the character in the Christmas story, and to think about the wider implications of the story.

Be imaginative and creative together is preparation for the next section. It allows some degree of poetic licence as you think about how the Christmas story might take place if it were to happen in your own community now. Suggested topics of discussion are given, but you do not have to be limited to these.

Born in my town – Jesus' birth in the twenty-first century enables you to enter into the relevance of the Christmas story to the *here and now* by portraying the story imaginatively, beginning in your own village, town or city, and culture. You can do this creatively by producing, for example, a play, poem, story or series of paintings or models for Advent, to be built up on a daily basis. A sample story is given which can be used as a guide, if required.

Pray together consists of two simple prayers: the first focuses on preparing ourselves for Christmas; the second looks at some of the people in need in the world this Christmas time. These prayers may be used as they are, adapted, added to or substituted.

Follow the maker's instructions relates the study of the twelve characters to some important passages in the Bible which look at how we should live our lives in preparation for the second coming of Jesus.

In the Christmas story links the character studied in the previous session with the theme.

Theme highlights what the session is about.

Read together gives the references for the Bible passage.

Chat together consists of some discussion points which will encourage you to chat informally about the **Theme** of the session.

Pray together is a personal response to the session, particularly seeking God's help in sharing the love of Jesus with others. This is given in the form of a few suggestions which may or may not be used.

Now be imaginative and creative together is all about producing a 'To Do' list in an imaginative and creative way. This should be placed somewhere prominent where it will be seen and acted upon. Some suggestions are listed, which may or may not be relevant to you. This may be worked on individually, in pairs or all together.

1 December
Gabriel

Then the angel told Mary,
'Don't be afraid! God is pleased with you,
and you will have a son.
His name will be Jesus.'
Luke 1:30, 31

Theme

God reveals his purposes.

Read together

Luke 1:26-33

Chat together

- One of the themes that we see running through the Bible is that God wants to communicate with us, his people, to reveal his purposes, and that's exciting! At the beginning of the Christmas story, God uses the angel Gabriel to deliver his message to Mary. In other parts of the Bible God communicates to people in dreams, including in the Christmas story (see Matthew 1:20 and 2:12). What other methods do you think God uses to speak to us today?
- Talk about why you want or need to communicate with friends and family. Why do you think God wants to communicate with us? Not everyone listens to God. Why do you think that is? Would people be more likely to listen to God if he sent an angel to them, as in the Christmas story? Maybe he has done: look at what it says in Hebrews 13:2.

Be imaginative and creative together

- Marriage and the family unit are important in the Christmas story. If the story was unfolding in your village, town or city in the twenty-first century, how and where do you think Joseph might propose to Mary?
- What job do you think Joseph might be doing? What are the main industries in your area, or do most people commute?
- Talk about modern methods of communication – for example, mobile phones and email. Despite all these ways of passing on messages to people, I think God would still send a personal messenger to announce the birth of his Son, don't you?

Born in my town – Jesus' birth in the twenty-first century

Mary lived in a small flint cottage with her mum and dad, on the outskirts of (*your village/town/city*). Life was good: she had recently left school, managed to get a good job with a local estate agent and was engaged to Joseph – a taxi driver. He had proposed to her over a bag of chips, sitting on the bench next to the taxi rank. But let's not get side-tracked. One evening, while Mary was waiting for her fiancé to arrive, her life was about to change for ever. Mary was in the lounge, sitting on a stool in front of the computer screen – her mum and dad were not home from work – when suddenly she was aware she was no longer alone.

'Mum? Dad?' She turned round to see an unknown figure sitting on the old rocking chair. 'Who . . .?'

'Don't look so worried,' the figure reassured. 'I've brought you some good news.'

Mary looked at the kind and radiant face of the figure – God's messenger. Her fears left her, immediately.

'You're going to have a baby; and he will be called Jesus.'

Drama
Poem
Painting
Model
The choice is yours . . .

Pray together

Almighty God,
thank you that you want to communicate with us all
this Christmas time.
Please teach us what the Christmas story means to today's world.
Help us to be good listeners to what you are saying to us
and to understand how we should apply those things to our daily lives.
In Jesus' name.
Amen.

Loving God,
thank you that you care about us all.
We pray for those who find it difficult to communicate with others
through disability or sickness:
that you will help them to break through the barriers that restrict them.
We pray for those who struggle to find the right words
to say what they want to say:
that you will guide them.
We pray for those who feel unloved or uncared for
because no one seems to make the time to talk to them:
be with them and surround them with your love.
Please help us to say and do the right things as we communicate with others.
In Jesus' name.
Amen.

2 December

Gabriel

God said,
'Now we will make humans,
and they will be like us.'
Genesis 1:26a

In the Christmas story

Gabriel communicates God's purposes to Mary.

Theme

We are created in God's image for a purpose.

Read together

Genesis 1:26

Chat together

- When God created us, he created us to be like him in many ways: with a degree of sovereignty; to have creative skills; with the ability to love, to be loved and to relate to others; and with an inner sense of morality (our conscience). What responsibilities come with the second half of Genesis 1:26? Talk about your creative skills – remember things like cooking and gardening as well as art, writing, etc. Write a list of the different kinds of relationships that are part of your daily lives. In one sentence describe the purpose of our conscience. When we do things that are not pleasing to God it spoils our relationship with him. Discuss.
- What do you think are God's purposes for us? Why do you think he created us in his image? See Matthew 6:33, John 4:34 and Philippians 3:14 for some ideas.

Pray together

- Ask for guidance as you prepare today's 'To Do' list.
- You may need to pray that God will show you clearly what your creative abilities are and how you can use them for him and for the benefit of others.
- Maybe you need help with relationships at home, at school, in your neighbourhood, at church. Relationships are never easy!
- You might want to pray that God will help you to know the right thing to do when faced with decisions.
- Perhaps you want to experience a closer relationship with God.
- And anything else that you feel led to pray about.

Now be imaginative and creative together

'To Do' list

Using your imagination and creative skills make a model or collage of an angel; leave a space somewhere to write your list.

- Maybe there is someone whom you have fallen out with, or someone you used to be close to whom you have lost touch with. Perhaps this Christmas is the time to write, phone or email.
- Do you have a creative talent that needs to be made use of in some positive way? What is it? How do you plan to make good use of it?
- Are there ways in which you could improve your relationship with God?

3 December

The Holy Spirit

The angel answered,
'The Holy Spirit will come down to you,
and God's power will come over you.
So your child will be called the holy Son of God.'
Luke 1:35

Theme

The Holy Spirit enables God's plan to be fulfilled.

Read together

Luke 1:34-35

Chat together

- In the Christmas story, it is the Holy Spirit who enables God's plan to be fulfilled. It is through his power that the miracle of God is worked and Jesus is born to Mary. God is the God of miracles. Discuss. Choose one or two favourite miracles from Mark's Gospel to look at and chat about.
- The Trinity is a difficult concept to even begin to understand. But what is easy to understand is that God the Father, Jesus the Son and the Holy Spirit share the same nature and purposes. They are united in everything they do. The Christmas story demonstrates this. What do you understand to be the nature of God? What does the word 'unity' mean?

Be imaginative and creative together

- Mary has just been told that she is going to have a baby. Talk about how you think she might be feeling after this sudden and unexpected news.
- Do you think it might change her reaction when Mary hears that the baby is to be the Son of God? In what way might it change?

Born in my town – Jesus' birth in the twenty-first century

Mary sat down on the old leather armchair, shocked and surprised by the angel's news.

'I don't understand,' she challenged. 'I can't be having a baby.'

Gabriel smiled at her reassuringly. 'God has chosen you to have a very special child: his own Son. This will all come about through the power of the Holy Spirit. Don't worry.'

Mary sat very still for what seemed like hours, but it was probably only a few minutes. Then she leaned forwards in the chair and clapped her hands together in nervous excitement.

'A child,' she mumbled to herself. 'God's Son!'

Drama
Poem
Painting
Model
The choice is yours . . .

Pray together

Almighty God,
thank you for the miracle of Christmas:
the birth of your Son, Jesus.
Thank you that when he grew up he lived among ordinary people,
working wonderful miracles and teaching more about you and your plans.
Thank you that he gave his life for us,
you raised him from the dead
and he is alive today.
Help us to make a positive response to the miracle of Christmas.
In Jesus' name.
Amen.

Loving God,
we pray for those in the world
who have not heard the true Christmas message:
who either know nothing at all about Christmas
or believe that it is just about buying presents
and eating too much rich food.
Please enable them to hear it.
In Jesus' name.
Amen.

4 December

The Holy Spirit

'But the Holy Spirit will come upon you and give you power.
Then you will tell everyone about me in Jerusalem,
in all Judea, in Samaria and everywhere in the world.'
Acts 1:8

In the Christmas story

The Holy Spirit enables God's plan to be fulfilled.

Theme

The Holy Spirit is the power to live out the Christian life of love and witness.

Read together

Acts 1:8

Chat together

- The wonderful thing about Acts 1:8 is that the challenge contained is preceded by a promise that will enable its fulfilment. What does that say about the nature of Jesus?
- In Matthew 5:13-16, Jesus tells us to be salt and light. What do you understand by that? Talk about the Ten Commandments (Exodus 20:1-17). As we study the teaching of the Bible, it can be very daunting as we try to live out the Christian life. How does it feel to know that God will give us the power through the Holy Spirit to be the kind of people and do the kind of things that are in line with the teaching of the Bible? Remember, though: it still isn't easy.

Pray together

- Ask for guidance as you prepare today's 'To Do' list.
- You may want to pray about times when you struggle to do or say the right thing.
- Perhaps you need to ask for strength and guidance in those difficult situations that come your way.
- Maybe you need to pray that you will experience the life-changing power of the Holy Spirit yourself.
- And anything else you feel led to pray about.

Now be imaginative and creative together

'To Do' list

Draw or paint a still life picture of a salt pot or mill, a light bulb or torch, and two pieces of rock as you would imagine were used for the Ten Commandments. Among all of this, leave a space to write your list.

- Perhaps you need to make more time to read what the Bible says about the way that we should live and how the Holy Spirit can help us. Remember that Jesus is our example.
- There can be times when we are reluctant to allow the Holy Spirit to guide or change us. Maybe that is something that needs to be addressed on your list.
- Perhaps you need to make time for chatting together regularly as a family about the things that concern you or things you are struggling to cope with.

5 December

Mary

Mary said,
'I am the Lord's servant!
Let it happen as you have said.'
Luke 1:38a

Theme

Mary is willing to serve.

Read together

Luke 1:36-38

Chat together

- God has called Mary to perform an incredibly special task. What is it? Her response is one of willingness to serve.
- With this calling, suddenly Mary's whole life is changing. In what ways might she expect things to be different? What kind of things will she need to do in preparation for the arrival of the baby? (Bear in mind that some things would have been very different in those days.)

Be imaginative and creative together

- Talk about the ways in which we prepare for a birth in the twenty-first century. Think about the colours and styles of baby products on sale. What would be your choice of colour for Jesus' nursery?
- How do you feel about change? What kind of changes don't you like? What kind of changes do you enjoy and maybe find exciting?

Born in my town – Jesus' birth in the twenty-first century

It had been an unexpected piece of news, to say the least. Mary stood up and began to walk around the small room, muttering to herself.

'I've got nothing ready – not even a cot. I'll need to write a shopping list: cot, pram, car seat, babygrows, nappies, bottles . . .' She hurried into the kitchen for a glass of water. 'There's so much to do . . . and what shall I say to Joseph?' The angel looked on, as Mary perched herself on the stool once again and sighed contentedly. 'All right, I'll do it.'

Mary grinned: she had assumed that she could have said 'no' if she really hadn't been prepared to be part of God's plan for her.

The angel Gabriel paused before leaving. 'And your cousin Elizabeth is having a baby too!'

Drama
Poem
Painting
Model
The choice is yours . . .

Pray together

Almighty God,
thank you for the example of Mary.
As we prepare for Christmas, please help us to be focused on Jesus
and let us not become distracted by the glitter and commercialism
that surrounds this time of year.
Help us to learn from Mary's willingness to serve you
and be part of your plan for her life.
In Jesus' name.
Amen.

Loving God,
thank you for all the good gifts that you shower us with.
Please help us to remember those who are poor, hungry, homeless,
thirsty, sick, lonely or bereaved this Christmas.
Fill us with the love of Jesus to share with those around us.
In his name we pray.
Amen.

6 December
Mary

Together you are the body of Christ.
Each one of you is part of his body.
1 Corinthians 12:27

In the Christmas story

Mary is called by God and expresses her willingness to serve.

Theme

We are part of the body of Christ.

Read together

1 Corinthians 12:12-31

Chat together

- Mary's calling involves preparing for the first coming of Jesus. As we prepare for his return, we are called to be part of the body of Christ. It is an interesting analogy: after Jesus' return to heaven (Acts 1:9) it is necessary for his followers to become his hands, feet and voice to continue his work here on earth. Talk about the importance of each part of our bodies, and what happens if a particular part fails to function. What happens if the messages from the brain don't reach their destination? How do these concepts relate to our calling to serve as part of the body of Christ?
- Think about your talents and abilities. Are you an up-front person or do you work away quietly in the background? Do you have leadership skills? Are you good with your hands? Which part of the body would you compare yourself to?

Pray together

- Ask for guidance as you prepare today's 'To Do' list.
- Pray that God will reveal to you the talents he has given you, and how he wants you to make use of them.
- Maybe you need to ask God to give you a willingness to serve and fulfil your calling as part of the body of Christ.
- Perhaps you seek to be enabled to work together with other followers of Jesus in being the hands, feet and voice of Jesus.
- God will give us the compassion and humility to put the needs of others before ourselves, when we ask. Maybe that's something you feel is needed in your life.
- And anything else you feel led to pray about.

Now be imaginative and creative together

'To Do' list

On a sheet of paper, draw the outline of a person and cut it out. This is what today's list will be written on.

- Perhaps you feel that you need to work at your talents and abilities to develop them – maybe take music or painting lessons, for example.
- Do you need to find out where your talents and abilities could be best used?
- Maybe there is someone close to you, whom you know needs your help.

7 December
Joseph

After Joseph woke up,
he and Mary were soon married,
just as the Lord's angel had told him to.
Matthew 1:24

Theme

Joseph is prepared to do things God's way.

Read together

Matthew 1:18-25

Chat together

- It must have come as quite a surprise when Joseph found out that Mary was pregnant. We are told that he was working out how he could call off all the wedding plans, in such a way that Mary would not be publicly disgraced. How do you think Joseph must have felt at the time? But when the angel appears to Joseph in a dream, everything changes. In what way? Why?
- Joseph agrees to do things God's way. Sometimes we don't understand why God chooses to do certain things in the way he does – but he knows best. Talk about why God knows best. If you can, give some examples of situations when, looking back, you have been able to understand why God acted in the way that he did.

Be imaginative and creative together

- What are the outward symptoms of feeling stressed or anxious? Talk about the kind of things that affect people in this way. If you feel able, share some of the things you get stressed about.
- Talk about dreams. Why do you think God might choose to speak to people in dreams?

Born in my town – Jesus' birth in the twenty-first century

It had been a long and stressful day. Joseph had just heard that his fiancée was pregnant – and the child wasn't his. To say that he was devastated was an understatement . . . although Mary had begged him to believe that she had done nothing wrong. As Joseph sat in his taxi waiting for another fare, he planned how he could call the marriage off without causing a public scandal. Sighing deeply, he lay his head back against the headrest, feeling himself drifting off to sleep. Moments later, loud snoring penetrated the half-open window.

'Joseph! Joseph!'

The taxi driver looked up in surprise to see an angel leaning against the car door. Joseph pressed a button and the window opened fully.

'I've got a message for you from God,' the angel told him. 'It's about Mary. The baby is God's Son, so don't call off the marriage plans . . . and when he is born you must call him Jesus.'

At that moment there was a loud bang on the taxi window. Joseph woke up with a start.

'Sorry, sir, you'll have to wait for the next taxi: I've got a wedding to organise.'

Drama
Poem
Painting
Model
The choice is yours . . .

Pray together

God of love,
thank you for loving each one of us,
and that as an expression of your love
you desire to give us good gifts.
Thank you that in your wisdom and knowledge you know what is best.
Please grant us the patience to wait for your perfect timing
and the faith to accept what we do not understand in your plans and purposes –
just like Joseph.
Strengthen our faith this Christmas, we pray.
In Jesus' name.
Amen.

Heavenly Father,
be with those who are struggling at this time
with difficult situations or damaged relationships.
Please offer your strength, love, wisdom, guidance and hope.
In Jesus' name.
Amen.

8 December

Joseph

Jesus walked on a little way.
Then he knelt with his face to the ground and prayed,
'My Father, if it's possible,
don't make me suffer by making me drink from this cup.
But do what you want, and not what I want.'
Matthew 26:39

In the Christmas story

Joseph agrees to do things God's way.

Theme

We should follow Jesus' example in doing God's will.

Read together

Matthew 26:36-46

Chat together

- Let's not pretend that, because Jesus is the Son of God, the suffering he is about to endure as he faces the cross is going to be any less real. Jesus prays that he might be excused this ordeal. Think of some hypothetical situations that you might choose to avoid. But Jesus concludes by emphasising that his Father's will should be done. How easy is it to pray that prayer when you are going through a difficult or painful situation?
- Do you sometimes ask for things in your prayers, which God answers with a firm 'No'? It is when a flower dies that the seed is produced. Through Jesus' death and resurrection we can be forgiven for the things that we have done wrong. Sometimes we need to go through hard times and experiences for something good to emerge. Discuss, sharing personal experiences if you feel able.

Pray together

- Ask for guidance as you prepare today's 'To Do' list.
- Talk to God about situations you are going through at the moment that you are struggling with.
- Remember that, even if God chooses not to remove that situation from you, he can strengthen and guide you – ask him.
- Pray for others who suffer: those who are sick, people suffering from loneliness or bereavement, the homeless, those who are hungry or have no clean water to drink.
- And anything else that you feel led to pray about.

Now be imaginative and creative together

'To Do' list

On a sheet of paper, draw the outline of a cross and cut it out. This is what today's list will be written on.

- Maybe your prayers need to include the clause 'Your will be done'.
- Is there a family member, teacher or close friend whom you can really trust? Sometimes it is good to speak to someone like that about problems and difficulties that you are going through.
- There might be something that you can do to help relieve the suffering of others.

9 December

God

No one has ever seen God.
The only Son, who is truly God and is closest to the Father,
has shown us what God is like.
John 1:18

Theme

God is the Father of Jesus.

Read together

John 1:1-18

Chat together

- John 1:18 states that no one has ever seen God but that Jesus shows us what he is like. Discuss this with reference to the teaching, stories, example and life of Jesus.
- Talk about family likenesses. In what ways are we already like God (see Genesis 1:27), and in what ways can we become more like God? How do we achieve that?

Be imaginative and creative together

- How would you feel about being given the task of parenting God's Son?
- What kind of special responsibilities might accompany such a calling?

Born in my town – Jesus' birth in the twenty-first century

As Joseph hurried round to find Mary, so that they could finish off making the arrangements, he recalled the words of the angel in his dream. He probably would have chosen a different name for the child, but . . . God's Son! What a huge responsibility.

'We need to go out and buy a cot,' he mumbled to himself. 'And I bet it will be a flat-pack as well.' He grinned, 'Never mind, I'll get Mary to help – she's always been good at DIY!'

Drama
Poem
Painting
Model
The choice is yours . . .

Pray together

Father God,
thank you that you sent your Son Jesus as a baby,
to grow up and live among us,
so that we might learn more about you.
Please give us a real hunger
to spend time discovering more about Jesus
through the Bible and our relationship with him.
Empower us, through your Holy Spirit, to be more like you.
In Jesus' name.
Amen.

Our loving heavenly Father,
thank you that you long for people to want to know more about you.
This Christmas time, within those who turn their back on you
please grant the desire to seek you through Jesus.
In his name.
Amen.

10 December
God

Jesus also told them another story:
Once a man had two sons.
Luke 15:11

In the Christmas story
God is the Father of Jesus.

Theme
God is our Father.

Read together
Luke 15:11-32

Chat together
- In general terms, talk about the imperfections of human parents – despite most of them trying their best. Include topics like role models, moral examples, trust and safety, dependability. Contrast with the fact that God is the perfect parent.
- The father in the Bible reading illustrates many of the qualities of God – our heavenly Father. Look through the passage and list them as they appear. Talk about these qualities. How does this story relate to us today? Which of the two sons is most like you, and why?

Pray together
- Ask for guidance as you prepare today's 'To Do' list.
- Pray for families: that parents will be given wisdom; for the healing of broken and damaged relationships; and for trust, safety and love within the home.
- Remember to pray for your own family . . . and yourself.
- You may need to ask for forgiveness – that will involve saying 'sorry'.
- You may need to ask for help to forgive someone who has hurt you.
- Prayerfully open up your life to God's love and ask for his help in sharing it with others.
- And anything else that you feel led to pray about.

Now be imaginative and creative together

'To Do' list

Make a 'Welcome Home' card. If you are feeling adventurous, you might like to try something like quilling or decoupage. Open up the card and write today's list inside.

- Is there anyone you have fallen out with, with whom you need to make contact – maybe a bunch of flowers or some other small gift might help?
- Perhaps there is a lack of respect and co-operation in your family that needs addressing.
- Have you drifted away from God like the lost son? If so, what are you going to do about it?
- Maybe you are bearing resentment or jealousy, like the lost son's brother. Don't let it fester.

11 December

Innkeeper

And while they were there,
she gave birth to her firstborn son.
She dressed him in baby clothes
and laid him on a bed of hay,
because there was no room for them in the inn.
Luke 2:6, 7

Theme

The innkeeper makes room for Jesus.

Read together

Luke 2:1-7

Chat together

- Is it sufficient that the innkeeper has pulled out all the stops and found an alternative venue for Mary and Joseph (and Jesus)? Or should he have made room somewhere in the inn? It has been suggested that maybe the innkeeper's wife intervened, asking for a more charitable spirit, and as a result the animal shelter was made ready. At Christmas time we hear so much about people getting into debt, overeating, drink-driving, late night parties. It is so easy to find that the busyness and commercialism of Christmas pushes Jesus out. What do you think? Give some examples of ways in which this happens in your community. How and where do you intend to fit Jesus into your Christmas?
- God allows Jesus' birth to take place in very humble surroundings. Jesus wants to be involved in our lives, our families and our homes. We don't need to be rich, powerful or famous to qualify. He accepts us as we are. Discuss.

Be imaginative and creative together

- Think about how you would prepare to go on a long journey. How would you travel? What would you take with you? What precautions might you think about?
- In what humble surroundings do you think the baby Jesus would be born in the twenty-first century?

Born in my town – Jesus' birth in the twenty-first century

Joseph and Mary hadn't been married for long, when a very official letter popped through the letterbox on to the door mat. It was a large envelope and covered up the LCOM in 'WELCOME'.

'I don't . . .' Joseph fumed. 'It couldn't have come at a worse time.'

Mary poked her head round the door. 'I'm just making a pot of tea: would you like some?'

'Just coming.'

As they sat down at the breakfast bar Joseph spread the letter out.

'The government is conducting a census, and I have to go down south to where I was born.' Joseph hesitated. 'When I say "I" I mean "we".'

Mary looked anxious. 'What about the baby?'

Joseph shrugged his shoulders. 'We've no choice. I'll take you down in the taxi; we'll find somewhere nice to stay . . . and there are some good hospitals down there. Don't worry.'

She rubbed her bulging tummy. 'We've got to take care of little Jesus.'

Joseph staggered to the car under the weight of luggage.

'We ought to take a packet of nappies, some babygrows, bottles, baby milk . . .' Mary frowned as she inspected the grubby interior of the old taxi. 'Just in case . . . You know, you really ought to have cleaned the seats and carpets.'

'We need to go now, love.'

It was while Joseph was repairing a puncture on the way that Mary suddenly queried, 'You did book up on the internet for us to stay somewhere, didn't you?'

'Everywhere was booked up, but I'm sure we'll find somewhere when we arrive.'

And so that night Joseph and Mary snuggled up on mattresses in a double garage behind the Crown Inn. And that was where the birth took place thanks to a helpful midwife staying at the inn – the heavy traffic had delayed the ambulance and prevented Joseph from getting Mary to the hospital in time.

'Good job I brought the Moses basket,' Mary said, as they awaited the late arrival of the ambulance.

Drama
Poem
Painting
Model
The choice is yours . . .

Pray together

Lord Jesus,
thank you that you want to be part of our lives, our families and our homes.
Please help us to make room for you,
not just in the busyness of Christmas but all the time.
Protect us from the temptations at this time of year
to over-spend and over-indulge in ways that are not helpful or healthy.
Amen.

Loving heavenly Father,
thank you for the coming of Jesus,
for all that he did and said during his life on earth,
and that he died for us on the cross – and rose again.
Thank you that Jesus is alive today,
bringing peace and hope to troubled lives.
Amid the materialism of our modern society at this time of year,
please open people's hearts and minds to what Christmas is really about:
meeting with your Son, Jesus.
In his name we pray.
Amen.

12 December
Innkeeper

Jesus replied,
'If you want to be perfect,
go and sell everything you own!
Give the money to the poor,
and you will have riches in heaven.
Then come and be my follower.'
Matthew 19:21

In the Christmas story
The innkeeper makes room for Jesus.

Theme
Priorities and idols distract us from following Jesus.

Read together
Matthew 19:16-30

Chat together
- Things that distract us from following Jesus come in many different forms. Talk about the reasons people give for not committing to being an active part of the church today. Which do you consider to be valid reasons, and which involve incorrect priorities? What is peer pressure, and how can that distract us from living according to Jesus' teaching and example?
- Jesus tells the man in the Bible passage to sell all that he has, give the money to the poor and then follow him. The problem is that the young man has made his money and possessions into idols or gods, and failed to use his wealth in a generous or responsible way. His whole life appears to have revolved around worshipping material objects. In society today we see so much evidence of greed, materialism, addictions, vanity, selfish ambition, and immoral lifestyles. Anything which is contrary to biblical values, or prevents the Triune God (God the Father, Jesus the Son and the Holy Spirit) from taking first place in our lives is unacceptable. Discuss.

Pray together
- Ask for guidance as you prepare today's 'To Do' list.
- Pray that God will reveal to you anything that you need to give up in your life.
- Seek God's guidance regarding any resources that you could put to better or more generous use.
- Ask God to enable you to make any necessary changes in your life following this session.
- And anything else that you feel led to pray about.

Now be imaginative and creative together

'To Do' list

In preparation for today's list, cut out some small rectangles from a sheet of coloured paper or thin card: approximately 2 x 10 centimetres. Write down aspects of your life that are important to you: each one on a separate piece of paper or card. Include things like family, school, work, hobbies, God. On a flat surface arrange the cards in order of their importance in your life. Then rearrange them into the order of priority which you feel they should have, with the Triune God at the top. Now stick them on a sheet of paper in that order, and write your list next to them.

- The 'To Do' list will consist of the changes you feel you need to make to your life in order to achieve the revised list of priorities.

13 December

The angel of the Lord

But the angel said, 'Don't be afraid! I have good news for you,
which will make everyone happy.
This very day in King David's home town
a Saviour was born for you. He is Christ the Lord.'
Luke 2:10, 11

Theme

The angel of the Lord passes on the good news.

Read together

Luke 2:8-14

Chat together

- How proficient are you at passing on good news to others? Sometimes we are more eager to pass on bad news or, worse still, gossip. Why do you think that is? What makes gossip so destructive? How does confidentiality slot into this? Talk about the good news that the angel has come to announce.
- The angel is anxious that the shepherds' fears do not prevent them from hearing the good news. Why are so many people today reluctant to listen to the good news of Christmas? Is it that they can't be bothered to listen, or are they afraid to face up to the implications of God sending his own Son into the world as a baby? What are the implications?

Be imaginative and creative together

- If the Christmas story were to take place today, where might God find a crowd of people late at night to send his angels to?
- By what means do you think the angel would appear, and what do you think the angel would look like? Remember, on this occasion God wants to create a bit of a splash!
- How do you think people would react?

Born in my town – Jesus' birth in the twenty-first century

Even at that late hour trains full of people were still arriving at the local station. Martin looked at his watch.

'What a night,' he sighed. 'In all my years of working for the railway, I've never known a time like it – all these extra trains!'

Over the loudspeaker he heard, 'The next train coming in at platform 3 . . .'

Martin braced himself for the rush: soon there would be people pushing and shoving, looking for taxis, asking the way to different hotels. The rumble of a large train could be heard coming into the station. Moments later the platform was heaving once again with travellers from far-off places. It was chaos . . . that is, until a dazzling light appeared in the middle of the busyness. A figure appeared in the centre of the light and began to speak. Although the figure looked ordinary in many ways, there was also something special that everyone could feel – a kind of holiness! Everyone gathered round, pushing to get to the front.

'What's happening?'

'Let me see!'

Then someone shouted, 'LISTEN, SO WE CAN HEAR WHAT IT'S ALL ABOUT.'

The angelic figure began to speak, 'Something really special has happened. A baby has been born, just up the road behind the Crown Inn.'

'A baby?' someone repeated. 'What's so special about a baby?'

'This is no ordinary baby,' the angel replied excitedly. 'This one has the power to save the world from people's wrongdoing and evil.'

Drama
Poem
Painting
Model
The choice is yours . . .

Pray together

Gracious God,
thank you for the truth and promise in the Christmas story.
Please let my response to its challenge be a positive one,
and give me the courage to pass on the good news to others.
In Jesus' name.
Amen.

Merciful God,
thank you for sending your messenger all those years ago to the shepherds,
to reveal to them the good news of the birth of Jesus.
Thank you that in the world today
human messengers are still sharing the Christmas story with others.
Please give their hearers the desire to stop and listen carefully
in the busyness of the Christmas period,
and motivate them to make a positive response.
In Jesus' name.
Amen.

14 December

The angel of the Lord

Go to the people of all nations and make them my disciples.
Matthew 28:19a

In the Christmas story

The angel of the Lord passes on the good news.

Theme

We are commissioned by Jesus to tell others.

Read together

Matthew 28:16-20

Chat together

- Acts 1:11 makes the promise that Jesus will return. In the meantime Jesus has left us with specific instructions for the task to be carried out. In the teaching of Jesus, there is a sense of urgency about the job in hand. We are called to spread the good news about him. Talk about ways in which we can speak to others about Jesus in words, actions and lifestyle.
- When we follow Jesus in faith, we are never on our own. In Matthew 28:20 Jesus promises always to be with us. It is a comforting promise and one which highlights the fact that we are not expected – or able – to fulfil our calling in our own strength. The parable of the growing seed (Mark 4:26-29) emphasises that without divine help our efforts will fail. Indeed, Acts 1:8 promises the power of the Holy Spirit. Discuss.

Pray together

- Ask for guidance as you prepare today's 'To Do' list.
- Pray for courage to speak to people about the message of Jesus – in words, actions and lifestyle.
- Seek guidance and strength from the Holy Spirit to make good use of the opportunities God gives.
- And anything else that you feel led to pray about.

Now be imaginative and creative together

'To Do' list

Buy a few bulbs and plant them in a pot. Care for them and watch the miracle of growth. Write your 'To Do' list on a sticky label which can be placed on the pot.

- Plan to tell the good news of Jesus to someone today.
- Write down the way in which you intend to do that.
- Perhaps there are good deeds that you feel you should be doing but are not.
- There could be changes that you feel you need to make in your own lifestyle, in order to live the kind of life that speaks to others about Jesus.

15 December

Shepherds

When the shepherds saw Jesus,
they told his parents what the angel had said about him.
Everyone listened and was surprised.
Luke 2:17, 18

Theme

The shepherds share their personal experience of Jesus with others.

Read together

Luke 2:15-20

Chat together

- One of the crucial features of being a witness is being willing to share personal experience of a situation with others. What is there in the Bible passage to suggest that the shepherds are eager to share their personal experience of this special night with others? Talk about the feelings that we see them experiencing.
- The shepherds return to their flocks. In some ways their lives remain the same, but in other ways their lives will never be the same again. Discuss.

Be imaginative and creative together

- Think back to the crowd at the train station. Who do you think might be most likely to go and visit the baby? Maybe it would be some of society's most vulnerable people. What do you think?
- What gifts might be taken to the new baby?
- How do you think the twenty-first-century media might be involved?

Born in my town – Jesus' birth in the twenty-first century

'Hey, mate . . . Did you hear that? Do you think that could apply to us?'

'In your dreams, son . . .'

Mark had been living on the streets since the autumn, after a bust-up with his family. He longed to be reunited with his mum but held out little hope. The father figures in his life had been physically abusive and poor role models. He couldn't see a way home, unless his mum was left on her own again.

Susan had suffered with depression for years. Life was a constant struggle as she slipped from highs into lows. She managed to cope on her own in a small bed-sit with extreme difficulty.

Roy was a company director. He was married with two children. The family could be described as comfortably off.

Joanne worked in the coffee kiosk on the platform. She had just left school and lived with her mum not far from the station.

Twenty-eight people set out together to search for the Son of God.

'Wait a minute,' Susan called out, reaching into her pocket for a two-pound coin. 'Let's just get a small toy from the late-night filling station on the way.'

She came out with a small teddy bear, dressed in the local football strip.

Roy looked concerned. 'Is it safe for a small baby?'

She read, 'Not suitable for children less than 3 years old.'

'Never mind,' Joanne concluded, 'the thought was there. Maybe it could be put on a shelf for him to look at.'

Mark knew where the Crown Inn was, and led the way. 'Over there!' he encouraged. 'The double garage is round the back.'

Everyone crept round on tip-toes, anxious not to wake the baby.

'Come in,' Joseph said in a loud whisper.

Everyone crowded in and stood in a semicircle around the Moses basket, completely overwhelmed by the whole situation.

Joanne explained to Mary and Joseph how they had come to be there. 'It was so exciting!'

Susan stepped forward and did a little curtsey. 'I've brought a small gift for him.' She pointed out the label.

Joseph took the small bear and thanked her. 'I don't want to hurry you, but I think I can hear the ambulance coming.'

Everyone went away eager to spread the good news. One of them had a friend who reported for the local press, so he sent a text on his mobile phone with the news.

Drama
Poem
Painting
Model
The choice is yours . . .

Pray together

Lord Jesus,
thank you that when we have put our faith in you,
we enter into a wonderful friendship that is worth telling others about.
Please motivate us and give us the courage
to share with others our personal experience of you
this Christmas and in the future.
Amen.

Heavenly Father,
we thank you that the Christmas message is for all people.
Please be with those who are lonely and vulnerable at this time.
Help them in their need
and draw them closer to you.
Let all those who need to hear the true message of Christmas this year
hear it through some means and respond positively.
In Jesus' name.
Amen.

16 December

Shepherds

'Go back home and tell everyone how much God has done for you.'
The man then went all over town,
telling everything that Jesus had done for him.
Luke 8:39

In the Christmas story

The shepherds share their personal experience of the birth of Jesus.

Theme

Testimony: sharing our personal experience of Jesus with others.

Read together

Luke 8:26-39

Chat together

- Talk about your personal experience of God, Jesus and the Holy Spirit. How would you feel about sharing it with others? What kind of things might you find off-putting in your attempt to witness in this way?
- Jesus tells the man in the story to go back home and tell everyone what God has done for him. Often, in the context of the good news of Christmas and our response to it, the people Jesus calls us to speak to, share with and be an example to are those with whom we live, socialise and work. Think about the different people you meet each day whom you could do this with.

Pray together

- Ask for guidance as you prepare today's 'To Do' list.
- We all need to ask for help to be the kind of example to others that Jesus intends us to be.
- Pray for new opportunities to share your experience of Jesus with others.
- Remember that God can help you to overcome barriers, if you ask him.
- Thank Jesus for all that he has done for you – and continues to do for you.
- And anything else that you feel led to pray about.

Now be imaginative and creative together

'To Do' list

Make a Christmas card depicting the shepherds visiting the baby Jesus, and write your list inside. Don't get it muddled up with your other cards because you will need to refer back to this one.

- You might feel it appropriate to plan ways in which your example to others might be improved.
- Jot down the name of someone with whom you would like to share something of your personal experience of Jesus today. Decide beforehand how you plan to do it.
- Write down some challenging ways in which you might make your walk with Jesus stronger.

17 December

Wise men

When the men went into the house and saw the child with Mary,
his mother, they knelt down and worshipped him.
They took out their gifts of gold, frankincense and myrrh
and gave them to him.
Matthew 2:11

Theme

The wise men bring a gift of gold.

Read together

Matthew 2:1-12

Chat together

- Some people, when choosing gifts for others, take the attitude that anything will do as long as it is quick to select and cheap; others spend ages, never counting the cost, striving to pick just the right gift for the right person. The wise men bring Jesus gifts that are very appropriate to his life and mission to humankind. What gift would you choose for Jesus, and why?
- The first gift that the wise men have brought is gold: appropriate for a king. Therefore, it is not really surprising that the wise men's first call is at Herod's palace. Talk about the contrast of a royal palace and the actual situation into which Jesus has been born. Why do you think this is?

Be imaginative and creative together

- What might be the modern equivalent of the three wise men? Remember that they follow a star.
- The wise men's journey is a long one. Matthew 2:11 states that the family have moved into a house by this time. What are the implications of this passing of time?
- Begin to think about the gifts that are brought to Jesus. What do you think might be an appropriate gift for a king today?

Born in my town – Jesus' birth in the twenty-first century

A group of astronomers, who had met together from all over the world for a conference in the Australian outback, were excitedly preparing to view the stars – in the absence of street lights . . . or any other lights, come to that. There was an air of eager anticipation as they set up their massive telescopes.

'It's a lovely clear night,' Peter commented.

Others agreed in a variety of different languages, as they began to view the stars.

'It's amazing: no lights to obscure things,' John commented.

He was from London . . . say no more! All of a sudden there was an excited squeal.

'What is it, Rachel?' Peter quizzed. 'Is there a spider crawling on the end of your telescope?'

The emotion welled up inside the 35-year-old science teacher. 'You're not going to believe this, but I think I have found a new star – and it's huge.'

Laptops were switched on as the astronomers searched for more information.

'In old manuscripts it is believed that the appearance of a new star signifies the birth of a king,' John read.

There was laughter in the background, but Peter, John and Rachel hastily began to pack up their things.

'Where are you three going?'

John grinned excitedly. 'We're going to the nearest internet access so we can find out if there has been a new king born anywhere . . . and then we're going visiting.'

'You must be joking!' someone shouted out.

But it was too late. The three astronomers hurried out towards their rented 4 x 4. It could be a long journey as they were backpacking around the world. Money was short, so they would have to get temporary jobs on the way.

In the meantime, Jesus, Joseph and Mary had moved into a house nearby. It was there that the group of backpacking astronomers eventually arrived – very tired. They had discovered from the internet that this baby was no ordinary baby. He was a king, but he was also the Son of God – the one that people had been expecting from their study of Scripture. Special thought and consideration had been needed as they had carefully chosen presents on the way.

'Please accept this gift,' Peter said as he presented the family with a small, carefully wrapped package.

The young Jesus tore the paper off excitedly to reveal a gold, jewel-studded photograph frame, in the shape of a heart.

'I'm sure that you will have lots of treasured memories which you will be able to capture on camera,' Peter explained to Mary and Joseph. 'As for the gold and the jewels: I don't suppose they're real at that price, but they're appropriate for a king. The heart shape seemed appropriate as well; after all, the best kingdoms must be ruled by love.'

Mary thanked them and smiled as she visualised one of the baby pictures sitting on the hall table in the golden frame.

Drama
Poem
Painting
Model
The choice is yours . . .

Pray together

Loving Jesus,
thank you that although you are the King of kings,
you still have time for me.
Please help me to make time for you in my life
and to do your work in serving others.
Amen.

Lord Jesus, King of kings,
thank you for demonstrating, in your birth and life on earth,
the nature of humility and servanthood.
Please help us to follow your example as we seek to serve others.
Thank you that you came to offer forgiveness, peace and hope to all people,
and not just the rich and powerful.
Please help people to respond in faith to your call to follow.
Amen.

18 December

Wise men

This story will show you what the kingdom of heaven is like:
One day a king decided to call in his officials
and ask them to give an account of what they owed him.
Matthew 18:23

In the Christmas story

The wise men give a gift that reflects the kingship of Jesus – gold.

Theme

The nature of the kingdom.

Read together

Matthew 18:21-35

Chat together

- As the nature of his birth would suggest, the kingdom that Jesus talks about in his ministry is based on very different values to those we might associate with typical kings and queens from history. Jesus uses the story in today's Bible reading as an illustration of what his kingdom is like. What particular aspect does the story bring out (N.B. verse 21)? Talk through what happens to the first person who is brought to the king? Who do you think the different characters represent?
- We have all done things wrong. This story highlights that through approaching Jesus in faith and saying 'sorry' – and really meaning it – we are forgiven. However, a warning is given (see also Matthew 6:14, 15). What is that warning? Discuss.

Pray together

- Ask for guidance as you prepare today's 'To Do' list.
- Maybe there are things that you need to say 'sorry' to Jesus for.
- If you find it hard to forgive others, pray that you will be filled with the love of Jesus to share with others and enable that forgiveness to take place.
- Don't forget to say 'thank you' to Jesus for the forgiveness he offers.
- Perhaps you could take this opportunity to say 'thank you' for other things that Jesus has done for you.
- And anything else that you feel led to pray about.

Now be imaginative and creative together

'To Do' list

Using some gold paper and a small box, make yourself a dummy bar of gold to write your list on.

- Write a reminder to say 'thank you' in your prayers, as well as 'please'.
- If you found yourself saying 'sorry' to Jesus, there may be a few things that you need to remember not to do again. The Holy Spirit can strengthen you.
- Perhaps there is a letter, email, text, telephone call or personal visit you need to make to express your forgiveness to someone – and begin to heal that relationship. It could be a good time to use a small gift!
- Maybe there's someone who has wronged you who is not prepared to make the first move to reconciliation – but perhaps you could!
- There might be someone whom you have wronged and to whom you need to apologise.

19 December

Wise men

When the men went into the house and saw the child with Mary,
his mother, they knelt down and worshipped him.
They took out their gifts of gold,
frankincense and myrrh and gave them to him.
Matthew 2:11

Theme

The wise men bring a gift of frankincense.

Read together

Matthew 2:1-12

Chat together

- The second gift that the wise men bring the baby Jesus is frankincense – a symbol of prayer, signifying his divinity. At the time of Jesus' birth, of course, the Scriptures consisted of the Old Testament only. But let's not forget that he is expected – the Old Testament prophets have been prophesying about Jesus' birth, life, death and resurrection for generations. That in itself makes him someone special. Discuss.
- The humanity of Jesus means that during his life on earth he experiences things like temptation, sadness, rejection, pain, suffering and tiredness. As for the divinity of Jesus, what better way for God to reveal himself and his purposes to us than by sending his Son to live here on earth? Look through one of the Gospels and find examples of passages that illustrate both aspects of Jesus; talk about their relevance to us today.

Be imaginative and creative together

- It's quite a challenge trying to think of modern equivalents of the gifts that the wise men bring in the Christmas story. What would someone give today that symbolised divinity?
- Try to imagine Jesus as an active and responsive toddler.

Born in my town – Jesus' birth in the twenty-first century

Rachel had quite taken to the toddler . . . and vice versa.

Putting one arm around him, she held out a small parcel, wrapped in teddy bear paper, with the other hand. 'This is something very special, just for you.'

He pulled at the paper, chuckling excitedly at this new game. Inside was a small brightly coloured Old Testament. 'When you get a little older you will be able to read this and learn more about your Father.'

Mary swallowed, touched by the kindness and knowledge of their visitors. 'I shall always remember your kindness.'

Joseph said little, but that was not to say that he wasn't taking in the significance of the whole event.

Drama
Poem
Painting
Model
The choice is yours . . .

Pray together

Lord Jesus,
thank you that you understand the things we go through.
Please help us to look to your example and the words of the Bible
as we face up to difficult situations in life.
Guide us and strengthen us during those times,
and renew our commitment to you this Christmas.
Amen.

Loving Father,
thank you for the birth of Jesus,
for allowing your Son to live on this earth,
in order to reveal more about yourself and your purposes.
Please help us and others to look to Jesus
and, in so doing, to learn from him
and respond in a positive way to his message.
Thank you for your undying, unconditional love for us
and for the way in which you provide for and sustain the world you created.
In Jesus' name.
Amen.

20 December

Wise men

Jesus replied:
'Philip, I have been with you for a long time. Don't you know who I am?
If you have seen me, you have seen the Father.
How can you ask me to show you the Father?'
John 14:9

In the Christmas story

The wise men give a gift that represents the divinity of Jesus – frankincense.

Theme

Learning more about God the Father through Jesus.

Read together

John 14:5-14

Chat together

- Jesus is surprised at Philip's request to be shown the Father. He tells him, 'If you have seen me, you have seen the Father.' The family likeness is far more than just a vague resemblance. Why, then, is it so important to study meticulously the life and teaching of Jesus?
- What do you understand about the nature of the Trinity? The important thing is to accept that God the Father, Jesus the Son and the Holy Spirit dwell in unity and fellowship with one another, and they share the same nature and purposes. Discuss.

Pray together

- Ask for guidance as you prepare today's 'To Do' list.
- Some things we don't fully understand. Some things we don't need to understand. In a sense, that is where faith comes in (see Hebrews 11:1). Maybe you need to ask God for more faith.
- Pray that you will experience the Triune God in all his fullness: the Fatherhood of God; the forgiveness and restoration that is only possible through Jesus; and the cleansing, guiding, strengthening and transforming power of the Holy Spirit.
- Be thankful again for the Triune God's goodness and endless expressions of love.
- Remember to pray for people who are lonely and vulnerable.
- And anything else that you feel led to pray about.

Now be imaginative and creative together

'To Do' list

Make a bookmark to use in your Bible. Use your imagination but remember to leave room for your list.

- Maybe there are ways in which you can experience the Triune God more fully – for example, spending more time in prayer and Bible study; striving to be more like Jesus and following him more closely; allowing the Holy Spirit to work fully in your life; and making more time to experience the fatherhood of God.

21 December

Wise men

When the men went into the house and saw the child with Mary,
his mother, they knelt down and worshipped him.
They took out their gifts of gold, frankincense and myrrh
and gave them to him.
Matthew 2:11

Theme

The wise men bring a gift of myrrh.

Read together

Matthew 2:1-12

Chat together

- The third gift that the wise men bring Jesus is myrrh, which is linked with death and burial. Indeed, the Old Testament Scriptures talk about the way in which the death of Jesus will take place. The wise men's gifts act as reminders that the Christmas story is not about a baby who is never heard of again: the birth of Jesus is just the beginning of a story that is still ongoing today – one of which we can be part. Discuss.
- Romans 8:28 tells us that God can bring good out of the most difficult and seemingly tragic situations. Can you think of some hypothetical examples of situations where this could be the case? Maybe you feel like sharing some of your own experiences as well. (But remember, sometimes, although good may have come from a situation, we might not have the opportunity to see or understand what it is.)

Be imaginative and creative together

- Think about the emotions that might arise when a gift is presented that symbolises death.
- How do you think the bearer of such a gift might approach the giving of it?

Born in my town – Jesus' birth in the twenty-first century

John was the last of the visitors to come forward. He felt apprehensive and sad because the gift he had brought was linked with the death of Jesus – it was a candle, scented with exotic herbs and spices.

'The light of the candle will symbolise living a life based on the light of love, truth, goodness and hope; but the fragrance of the candle contains herbs and spices that are associated with suffering and death.'

Those who were familiar with the Old Testament prophets would have been only too aware that Jesus' ministry on earth would lead to suffering and a premature but ultimately victorious death. With this gift, the celebrations were tainted with a degree of sadness.

Before they returned home, God spoke to the backpackers through a newspaper they were reading. He told them to be careful who they told about what they had experienced, because many in society would try to suppress Jesus' ministry.

Drama
Poem
Painting
Model
The choice is yours . . .

Pray together

Lord Jesus,
thank you that you were prepared to come to a world
that would eventually put you to death,
in order that we might be able to share with you
in your victory over sin and evil.
Please grant us faith and commitment as we seek to follow you.
Amen.

God of love,
thank you for allowing Jesus to come and live among us,
revealing more of you and your purposes,
even though you knew the way he would be treated.
Thank you for the light of love, truth, goodness and hope
that Jesus still brings into the world today.
Thank you that you are all-knowing, all-seeing and all-powerful
and, as such, you are able to see the wider picture –
and bring good even from apparently tragic situations.
Please let nothing that has been achieved in Jesus' life, death or resurrection be wasted.
In his name we pray.
Amen.

22 December
Wise men

We know what love is because Jesus gave his life for us.
That's why we must give our lives for each other.
1 John 3:16

In the Christmas story
The wise men give Jesus a gift that reflects his death – myrrh – but God can bring something good from even the most tragic happenings.

Theme
Jesus' death on the cross is a demonstration of true love and the victory over sin and evil.

Read together
1 John 3:16-18

Chat together
- Jesus demonstrates his love for us all in being willing to die on the cross for us, paying the penalty for our sin, so that through faith in him and repentance we might be forgiven (see Romans 3:21-31). How does it make you feel to know that Jesus – the Son of God – gave his life on the cross for you?
- Talk about the kind of love that enables a person to be prepared to give their own life for the benefit of others. Give some examples of this happening in the world today – for example, people in the emergency services.

Pray together
- Ask for guidance as you prepare today's 'To Do' list.
- Jesus gave his life for you: that has to demand a huge 'thank you'.
- Pray for more selfless love in the world today.
- Jesus will fill you with his love to share with others, if you ask him.
- It would be good to spend time in prayer for those people who, on a daily basis, place their lives on the line for others.
- And anything else that you feel led to pray about.

Now be imaginative and creative together

'To Do' list

Make a 'thank you' card for Jesus. Write a message inside together with today's list.

- 1 John 3:18 highlights that one way in which we can demonstrate selfless love is to help other people in practical acts of kindness – and not just talk about it. You might like to begin your list with some ideas of what good deeds you might be able to perform.
- Maybe you could commit to praying regularly for someone you know who is in a high-risk profession.
- Write down something about your response to what Jesus has done for you.

23 December
Jesus

Eight days later Jesus' parents did for him
what the Law of Moses commands.
And they named him Jesus,
just as the angel had told Mary
when he promised she would have a baby.
Luke 2:21

Theme
The birth of Jesus is the fulfilment of God's promise.

Read together
Luke 2:21

Chat together
- Do you know what it's like to have to wait for a promise to be fulfilled? Talk about promises. If you feel able to, share personal experience of promises being kept . . . or not.
- The arrival of the baby Jesus in Bethlehem is the fulfilment of God's promise to Mary through the angel Gabriel. However, Jesus is also the fulfilment of a far greater promise to all humankind, long waited through Old Testament times. Using a study Bible, find and discuss examples of the prophecy concerning the birth, life, death and resurrection of Jesus (for example, Matthew 12:17-21).

Be imaginative and creative together
- The birth of Jesus marks the fulfilment of God's promise to Mary, but also a wider promise to all humankind. Think about ways of incorporating this into the finish of your story, drama, poem, painting or model.

Born in my town – Jesus' birth in the twenty-first century
With the birth of a tiny baby, God's promise to Mary is fulfilled. With the birth, life, death and resurrection of Jesus, so too are most of the Old Testament prophecies concerning the coming of someone special who would make it possible for humankind to be set free from the consequences of sin (disobedience to God). However, some of the promises of Scripture are still to be fulfilled. And so the story continues . . .

Drama
Poem
Painting
Model
The choice is yours . . .

Pray together

Loving heavenly Father,
thank you that you value and love each one of us so much
that you enabled us, through faith in Jesus,
to be forgiven for all the things we have done wrong.
Thank you that the mission of Jesus
is all about things like forgiveness, freedom, truth, hope and love.
Please help us to be willing to be part of the ongoing story of Jesus.
In his name.
Amen.

Faithful heavenly Father,
thank you for all the wonderful promises contained in Scripture –
all of them for the good of your creation, which includes humankind.
Thank you that you are faithful in fulfilling those promises.
Please inspire people to read the Bible,
discover more about your promises
and respond to them.
Comfort those who have been hurt by the broken promises of other people,
and restore their trust.
In Jesus' name.
Amen.

24 December

Jesus

We are filled with hope, as we wait for the glorious return
of our great God and Saviour Jesus Christ.
Titus 2:13

In the Christmas story

The birth of Jesus fulfils God's promise.

Theme

Peace and hope to the world.

Read together

Titus 2:11-14

Chat together

- So many things in this world end up letting us down. The material objects that we work so hard to obtain eventually break, corrode, wear out or are destroyed. Even the people on whom we depend often end up letting us down in some way – and we them! Think of some examples. But we can depend on God, the knowledge that Jesus will return and that then more of the great promises in the Bible will be fulfilled. There lies our hope. Talk about Acts 1:6-11. What is the challenge contained in verse 8? What are the promises contained in this passage?
- Through faith in Jesus we are saved from the consequences of disobedience to God. In the knowledge of that, we are able to find inner peace. Talk about guilt, anger, bitterness, jealousy, greed and discontent; then contrast them with the inner peace that is talked about in Acts 10:36.

Pray together

- Ask for guidance as you prepare today's 'To Do' list.
- There is a lot of work to do and a sense of urgency about doing it. Acts 1:8 promises the power of the Holy Spirit: we certainly need his help if we are to fulfil Jesus' commission. That's something you might like to pray about.
- Maybe you still need to pray for help to believe the promises in Scripture, or to take that step of faith necessary to enter into a relationship with Jesus.
- Perhaps you have issues with things like anger, bitterness, jealousy or greed. If so, that's something to pray about, and maybe discuss with a church leader or Christian counsellor.
- Pray for the physical and spiritual needs of others.
- And anything else that you feel led to pray about.

Now be imaginative and creative together

'To Do' list

Luke 9:62 compares following Jesus with ploughing: we cannot afford to look back, we need to keep moving forwards with our eyes fixed on Jesus. Make a model, draw, paint or cut out a picture of horses or a tractor pulling a plough. Leave space for your list.

- Today your list will comprise two verses of Scripture: Acts 1:8 and Luke 9:62.
- And anything else that you may feel led to add.

25 December
Jesus

The Son of Man came to look for and to save people who are lost.
Luke 19:10

Theme
Meeting with Jesus this Christmas.

Read together
Luke 19:1-10

Born in my town – Jesus' birth in the twenty-first century
Summary
We have been spending time placing the Christmas story into a modern context – where you live – beginning in your town, village or city, because it is not just history. The story is just as relevant to you this Christmas as it was to society all those years ago. Indeed, its relevance applies to your town (or village or city), your neighbourhood, your street, your home and your life. The Christmas story is an ongoing one: Jesus grew up, taught, did wonderful miracles, gave his life on the cross for us, rose again and is alive today changing people's lives for the better.

In the story of Zacchaeus we see someone who is caught up with materialism: money and possessions. But those things have obviously failed to satisfy. When he meets with Jesus, his whole life is transformed for the better. The emptiness and pointlessness in his life is replaced with hope, joy, contentment, fulfilment and inner peace. And he discovers the joy of giving as he hands out money to the poor and those he has cheated in the past.

It is so easy to get caught up in the materialism of Christmas today and fail to meet with Jesus. But it doesn't have to be like that. You can meet Jesus in faith for the first time this Christmas. You can meet with Jesus afresh and renew your commitment to him this Christmas. You can make room for Jesus in the busyness of your life this Christmas. You can bring the gift of yourself in service to Jesus this Christmas. You can share Jesus with others this Christmas in your town, village or city . . . in your neighbourhood . . . in your street . . . and in your home. You can experience the love, peace, joy and fulfilment of God – through meeting with Jesus – this Christmas.

Chat together
- Today is the climax of your Advent journey: it's CHRISTMAS DAY! So what is your response to Jesus? Is it to meet with him for the first time, to renew your commitment to him, or to let Christmas pass by without taking any action? To make room for Jesus or to allow the busyness of life to take priority? To receive and share the love of Jesus with those around you, or to do nothing? To take on the challenge of Acts 1:8, or miss out on the privilege of serving the King of kings? The choices are yours!

Pray together

Today's prayer needs to include your individual personal responses to Jesus. Say the beginning and ending of the prayer together and then take it in turns to pray out loud (or silently together) to bring your own personal responses to Jesus.

Lord Jesus,
thank you for this special time – Christmas Day –
when we remember your coming to the world as a baby.
Thank you that you grew up,
taught us more about God and his purposes,
worked amazing miracles that demonstrated qualities of the kingdom,
that you died on the cross paying the penalty for sin,
rose again and are alive today.
As we think afresh about your coming this Christmas
and its relevance to our villages, towns or cities,
to our streets and neighbourhoods and to our lives,
and as we prepare for your return,
please . . .

(Pray your own personal responses at this point)

Please be with others at this time
and help them to discover that Christmas is all about you.
Encourage them to make positive responses
and give them a sense of urgency as they await your return.
Amen.

(You may like to finish by saying together the Lord's Prayer and a blessing.)